HAUNTED HISTORY

AARON BURR'S GHOST

and Other New York City Hauntings

by Megan Cooley Peterson

CAPSTONE PRESS
a capstone imprint

Capstone Captivate is published by Capstone Press, an imprint of Capstone.
1710 Roe Crest Drive
North Mankato, Minnesota 56003
www.capstonepub.com

Library of Congress Cataloging-in-Publication Data is available on the Library of Congress website.
ISBN: 978-1-4966-8372-4 (library binding)
ISBN: 978-1-4966-8423-3 (eBook PDF)

Summary: Aaron Burr was once the vice president of the United States. Now his ghost is said to stalk a restaurant in Greenwich Village in New York City. What other ghosts are lurking in the city's shadows? Discover the haunted places of one of America's most notable cities. Between these pages, readers will find just the right amount of scariness for a cold, dark night.

Image Credits
Alamy: ART Collection, 8, Pictorial Press Ltd, bottom middle 16; iStockphoto: Remy, bottom 14; Newscom: Glasshouse Images, 21, Ken Welsh, 6, UPI/Newscom, 22; Pixabay: dannysantos, (wood) design element, geralt, (paper) design element; Shutterstock: ComicSans, (smoke) Cover, design element, Cranach, 20, Creativa Images, bottom left 4, Dan Kosmayer, bottom left 16, Dino Osmic, 9, Everett Historical, 13, 19, top 23, 24, 26, 27, Felix Mizioznikov, 25, Ink Drop, (map) 28-29, Jayne Chapman, 7, Joe Therasakdhi, top 14, Kathy Hutchins, bottom right 5, Keith Levit, (bottom left) Cover, littlenySTOCK, 28, MeinPhoto, (top) Cover, Peter Dedeurwaerder, 11, Pit Stock, top 29, PrasongTakham, bottom 23, T photography, 17, tovsla, 10, TTstudio, bottom 29, Victoria Lipov, 5; Wikimedia: Gift of Dr. John E. Stillwell, (bottom right) Cover

Quote Sources
p.11, "Hunting ghosts at New York City's Morris-Jumel Mansion." CBS News, Oct. 31, 2019; p.12, "The Most Hair-Raising, Haunted Spots in NYC." Guest of a Guest, Oct. 3, 2019; p.15, "Terror on 10th street." New York Post, Oct. 28, 2012

Editorial Credits
Editor: Renae Gilles; Designer: Sara Radka; Media Researcher: Morgan Walters; Production Specialist: Katy LaVigne

All internet sites appearing in back matter were available and accurate when this book was sent to press.

Printed and bound in the USA.
PA117

TABLE OF CONTENTS

Words in **bold** are in the glossary.

THE GHOSTLY CITY THAT NEVER SLEEPS

New York City is often called "the city that never sleeps." Restaurants stay open late into the night. The subway system runs nonstop. It takes people wherever they need to go, day or night. Some say the city's ghostly residents are also busy from dusk until dawn.

Dutch settlers founded New York City in 1624. They called their settlement New Amsterdam. The British took the city in 1664. They renamed it New York. It is one of the most famous cities in the world. Many U.S. presidents, world leaders, and artists have lived there. Beyond the city's famous sites and bright lights, could **ghosts** be lingering? Learn about some of the reported ghostly happenings and decide for yourself!

New York City is known for its nightlife. Do the city's theaters, diners, and clubs also entertain ghosts?

WHO YOU GONNA CALL?

The *Ghostbusters* movies from the 1980s were filmed in New York City. Many famous city landmarks appear in the films. The characters hunt ghosts at the New York Public Library, the Statue of Liberty, and Washington Square Park.

CHAPTER 1

A GHOSTLY VICE PRESIDENT

Aaron Burr challenged Alexander Hamilton to a duel in Weehawken, New Jersey, in 1804.

Aaron Burr was the third vice president of the United States. He served alongside President Thomas Jefferson from 1801 to 1805. He also killed Founding Father Alexander Hamilton in a famous duel in 1804. Burr died in 1836 after suffering a **stroke**. Ever since, Burr's ghost has been spotted all over New York City.

17 BARROW STREET

In the 1790s, Burr served as attorney general of New York. Burr kept his horses at a carriage house at 17 Barrow Street. Today, the carriage house is a restaurant. And diners aren't the only guests who stop for a bite. Ghosts are also said to haunt the building, including Aaron Burr.

The restaurant also plays host to other ghosts. Other reported ghosts include a blacksmith and a woman in black. The blacksmith has been spotted on the upper floors. Workers believe he may have lived there. The woman in black floats down a staircase and then vanishes.

Today, many old carriage houses have been updated.

Diners at the restaurant are often treated to spooky entertainment. Dishes fly on their own. Burr's ghost has been seen tossing dishes too. Chairs are pulled out from under guests by invisible hands. Lights flicker. Picture frames on the wall tilt to one side by themselves.

BATTERY PARK

Burr was charged with **treason** in 1807. He was accused of trying to establish a new country. After being found not guilty, Burr became highly unpopular in the United States. He fled to Europe. He left behind his beloved daughter, Theodosia.

In June 1812, Burr returned to New York City. That December, Theodosia set sail from her home in South Carolina. She was going to visit her father. But her ship was lost at sea. Burr never saw or heard from her again. Some say his ghost still waits for his daughter.

FREAKY FACT

Some stories say Theodosia was captured by pirates. They made her walk the plank.

Ships could be lost at sea in the 1800s for many reasons, including storms, pirate attacks, and icebergs.

Battery Park faces New York Harbor. Many park visitors say they've seen Burr's ghost there. His ghost watches the water as if he's waiting for Theodosia's ship. One woman believes Theodosia's ghost may also be at the park, looking for her father. In the 2000s, the woman was on a ghost tour at the park. Suddenly, one of her earrings fell off. She believes Theodosia's ghost snatched it. It is rumored that Theodosia loved jewelry.

New York Harbor empties into New York Bay and the Atlantic Ocean. It is one of the world's largest natural harbors.

FREAKY FACT

Theodosia's ghost has been seen at the restaurant on Barrow Street. Guests claim she walks up and down the stairs.

MORRIS-JUMEL MANSION

In 1833, Burr married Eliza Jumel and moved into her mansion. Today, the house is a museum. Many visitors believe it's haunted. In 2017, ghost hunters were recording in Burr's former bedroom. They recorded a strange voice. No one can agree on what it said. Some think the voice said, "He doesn't love you." Others think it said, "They're going to laugh at you." Was it Burr speaking from beyond the grave?

CHAPTER 2
THE HOUSE OF DEATH

A brick townhome at 14 West 10th Street has been nicknamed the "House of Death." Rumors say more than 20 people died there. But no one knows for sure. Built in the 1850s, the home was originally a mansion. In the 1930s, the home was made into apartments. Some say the ghosts of former residents never left.

MARK TWAIN

American author Mark Twain is the house's most famous ghost. Twain lived there from 1900 to 1901. Visitors have seen his ghost near the first-floor staircase. The ghost was dressed in a white suit. Twain often wore a white suit when he was alive.

In the 1930s, Twain's ghost is said to have spoken to a mother and a daughter. He was sitting near a window. He looked at them and said, "My name is Clemens, and I has a problem here I gotta settle." Then his ghost disappeared. Mark Twain's real name was Samuel Clemens.

Mark Twain's most famous novels include *The Adventures of Huckleberry Finn* and *The Adventures of Tom Sawyer*.

FREAKY FACT

Jan Bartell wrote a book about her ghostly experiences. She finished *Spindrift* in March 1973. She died of a heart attack that June. Some say the ghosts from 10th Street caused her death.

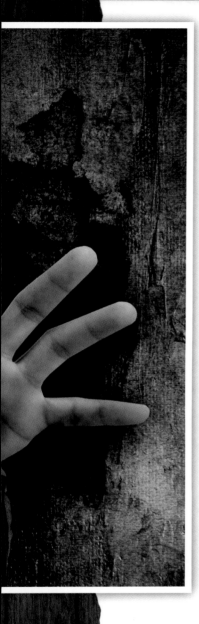

GET OUT

Actress Jan Bartell moved into one of the apartments in 1957. She was excited to settle into her new home. Her excitement ended soon after she moved in. Furniture moved on its own. Rapping sounds kept her awake at night. She said ghosts floated out of the walls. The ghosts made a terrible smell. Bartell told her landlord about the smell. He admitted that a dead body had been found in a wall. He wasn't sure how the body had ended up there.

Bartell invited a **medium** to her home to help. The medium sensed many ghosts there. Suddenly, one of the **spirits** took control of the medium. A ghostly woman said she was born in 1848. Her husband died in the U.S. Civil War (1861–1865). The ghost blamed President Abraham Lincoln for her husband's death. The medium asked the ghosts to leave the house. The ghostly woman shouted, "Never! I will never leave here!" Bartell moved out of the house.

CHAPTER 3

THE CHELSEA HOTEL

The Chelsea Hotel is one of New York City's most famous buildings. The hotel is also one of its most haunted. The hotel on West 23rd Street was built from 1883 to 1884. Many famous people lived there, including Mark Twain, Jimi Hendrix, and Madonna.

Dylan Thomas

FREAKY FACT

A woman claims she took a ghostly photo at the Chelsea in 2009. She believes a white spot in the photo is a ghostly skeleton.

At the time of its construction, the Chelsea Hotel was the tallest building in New York City.

ROOM 206

Poet Dylan Thomas spent his final days in Room 206 before his death in 1953. He fell into a **coma** in the room. Thomas was taken to a hospital, where he died. His official cause of death was **pneumonia**.

Thomas' ghost has been spotted at the hotel since his death. In 2009, a woman named Anna checked into Room 114. She slept well the first two nights. But on the third night, Anna saw a ghostly head floating in front of her mirror. The head looked like Thomas'.

MARY FROM THE FIFTH FLOOR

In 1912, a woman named Mary survived the sinking of the RMS *Titanic*. This famous passenger ship sank after hitting an iceberg. Mary's husband did not survive. After the sinking, Mary lived on the fifth floor of the Chelsea. She is said to have died in her room. Mary's ghost has been spotted on the fifth floor. Her ghost often looks at its reflection in a mirror.

In 1996, actor Michael Imperioli claimed he saw Mary's ghost at the Chelsea. One night, he returned to his room on the eighth floor. He saw a woman crying at the end of the hallway. Imperioli approached the woman. When he asked her what was wrong, a light bulb shattered. Then she vanished.

Only 706 of the 2,229 people on board survived the *Titanic's* sinking by getting into lifeboats.

CHAPTER 4

WASHINGTON SQUARE PARK

Washington Square Park has a dark past. The park was first used as a burial ground. Those who could not afford a proper burial were put to rest there. Then **yellow fever** swept through the city in 1797, 1798, 1801, and 1803. Even more bodies were buried in the park. More than 20,000 bodies may still be buried there. The ghosts of the dead are said to haunt the area. Visitors have reported seeing **orbs**. Ghost hunters believe ghosts can create these small balls of light. Ghostly children dressed in old-fashioned clothing also wander through the park.

FREAKY FACT

The Hanging tree stands 131.2 feet (40 meters) tall. It is estimated to be more than 300 years old.

Built in 1892, the arch in Washington Square Park was named for George Washington.

THE HANGING TREE

An English elm tree stands in the northwest corner of the park. **Legend** says it was used for hanging criminals. Some say you can see their ghosts hanging from the tree at night. Others argue that no one was ever hanged from that tree. Is it just a spooky story?

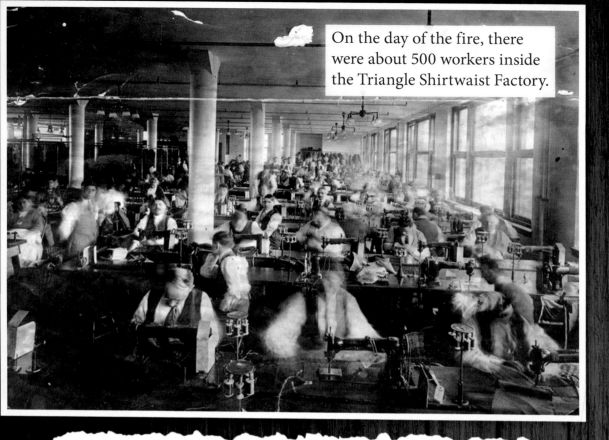

On the day of the fire, there were about 500 workers inside the Triangle Shirtwaist Factory.

TRIANGLE SHIRTWAIST FACTORY

The Triangle Shirtwaist Factory opened across from the park in 1900. The factory made women's shirts. In 1911, a fire broke out on the eighth floor. The doors were locked from the outside to stop workers from taking breaks or stealing. Workers could not escape when the fire broke out. Fire truck ladders weren't long enough to reach the trapped workers. Many jumped and fell to their deaths. At first, 154 people were feared dead. The fire killed 146 people, mostly women.

Today, the building is part of New York University. People say the building is haunted. The sound of women screaming and crying fills the halls. Witnesses smell smoke when there is no fire. One office worker may have seen a ghost outside the building. As the worker left, she saw a woman on the sidewalk. The woman looked confused. Her clothing was burned. The worker asked the woman if she needed help. The woman staggered around the corner and vanished.

PROTECTING WORKERS

The fire at the Triangle Shirtwaist Factory shocked America. New York State set up the Factory Investigating Commission. Its members studied the health and safety of many types of businesses. They wrote improved health and safety codes to keep workers safe. These included installing safer elevators and leaving factory doors unlocked during working hours.

23

CHAPTER 5

ELLIS ISLAND

From 1892 to 1954, 12 million **immigrants** passed through Ellis Island. If they were too sick, they were sent to the island's hospital. Once they were well enough, they could enter the United States. But some never left the hospital. As many as 3,500 people died there.

Today, the island's main building is open as a museum. Many people say it's haunted. Park rangers have heard children's voices. But when they investigated, there were no children there. Doors open and close on their own.

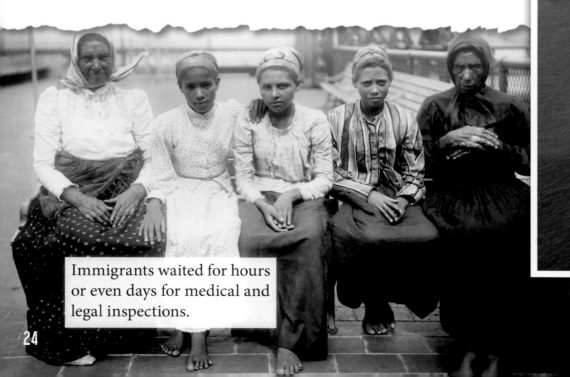

Immigrants waited for hours or even days for medical and legal inspections.

More than 3 million people visit Ellis Island every year.

main building (museum)

hospital

psychopathic ward

immigrant building

contagious disease wards

Canals of water once separated Ellis Island into three
different sections. Doctors hoped this would keep diseases
from spreading across the island and into New York City.

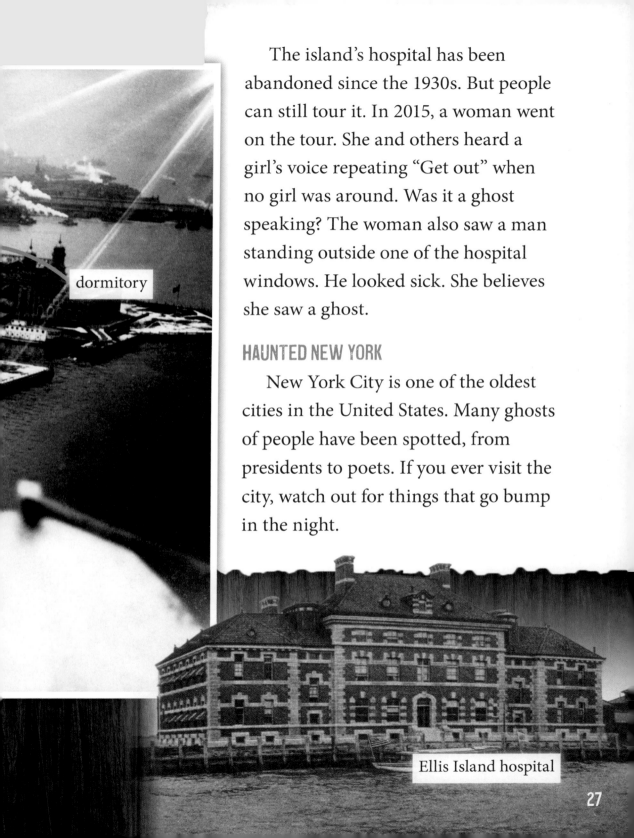

The island's hospital has been abandoned since the 1930s. But people can still tour it. In 2015, a woman went on the tour. She and others heard a girl's voice repeating "Get out" when no girl was around. Was it a ghost speaking? The woman also saw a man standing outside one of the hospital windows. He looked sick. She believes she saw a ghost.

HAUNTED NEW YORK

New York City is one of the oldest cities in the United States. Many ghosts of people have been spotted, from presidents to poets. If you ever visit the city, watch out for things that go bump in the night.

dormitory

Ellis Island hospital

Haunted Places of
NEW YORK

The Dakota

New Amsterdam Theatre

Grand Central Terminal

8. **Grand Central Terminal**

   A secret track below the station is said to be haunted. President Franklin D. Roosevelt often rode a secret underground train to a hotel in the city. People say the ghost of his dog, Fala, appears on the track.

9. **New Amsterdam Theatre**

   The ghost of former performer Olive Thomas is said to haunt this theater. She died in the 1920s.

10. **The Dakota**

    The ghost of musician John Lennon is said to haunt this apartment building. He died there in 1980.

GLOSSARY

coma (KOH-muh)—a state of deep unconsciousness from which it is very hard to wake up

ghost (GOHST)—a spirit of a dead person believed to haunt people or places

immigrant (IM-uh-gruhnt)—a person who leaves one country and settles in another

legend (LEJ-uhnd)—a story handed down from earlier times; legends are often based on fact, but they are not entirely true

medium (MEE-dee-uhm)—a person who claims to make contact with spirits of the dead

orb (AWRB)—a glowing ball of light that sometimes appears in photographs taken at reportedly haunted locations

pneumonia (noo-MOH-nyuh)—a serious disease that causes the lungs to become inflamed and filled with a thick fluid that makes breathing difficult

spirit (SPIHR-it)—the soul or invisible part of a person that is believed to control thoughts and feelings; some people believe the spirit leaves the body after death

stroke (STROHK)—a medical condition that occurs when a blocked blood vessel stops oxygen from reaching the brain

treason (TREE-zuhn)—the crime of betraying one's government

yellow fever (YEL-oh FEE-vur)—an illness that can cause high fever, chills, nausea, and kidney and liver failure; liver failure causes the skin to become yellow, giving the disease its name

READ MORE

Bingham, Jane. *Ghosts and Haunted Houses: Myth or Reality?* North Mankato, MN: Capstone Press, 2019.

Merwin, E. *Horror in New York.* New York: Bearport Publishing, 2020.

Owings, Lisa. *Haunted Houses.* Minneapolis: Bellwether Media, 2019.

INTERNET SITES

Aaron Burr, 3rd Vice President (1801–1805)
https://www.senate.gov/about/officers-staff/vice-president/VP_Aaron_Burr.htm

History of Ghost Stories
https://www.history.com/topics/halloween/historical-ghost-stories

New York Folklore
https://www.americanfolklore.net/folklore/united-states-folklore/new-york-folklore

INDEX